P9-ECO-525

Pilgrim's Regress

Pilgrim's Regress

cartoons from the pages of
The Critic
by
Bill Tidy
Charles Healy
Joseph Farris
Rodrigues
Sidney Harris

edited by
Joel Wells

The Thomas More Press
Chicago, Illinois

Copyright© 1979 by the Thomas More Association.

All rights reserved. Printed in the United States of America. No part of this publication may be reproduced, stored in a retrieval system, or transmitted, in any form or by any means, electronic, mechanical, photocopying, recording, or otherwise, without the written permission of the publisher, The Thomas More Association, 180 N. Wabash Avenue, Chicago, Illinois 60601.

ISBN 0-88347-093-4

Contents

Introduction, 7
Bill Tidy, 11
Charles Healy, 35
Joseph Farris, 59
Rodrigues, 83
Sidney Harris, 105

Introduction

Oh for the life of a cartoonist! Freed from the enervating coils
of the daily grind, they have only to move about observing the
great circus of contemporary inanity and then retire to their
comfortably appointed studios to dash off a few well-practiced
sketches; another few minutes to post the results off to affluent
magazines hungry for their work and then settle back to await
a bountiful green harvest from the mailbox.

Frankly, I stand in envious awe of cartoonists. Beside this
halcyon lifestyle must be placed the quiet satisfaction drawn
from the adulation of the ever-swelling army of one's fans, the
scarcely concealed admiration and open deference of people
one meets at parties when they realize just who it is indeed that
they are face to face with. Not to mention the secret sense of
power one holds over those who know that they must watch
what they say and do in front of you lest their foolishness
become grist for your mill and they find themselves penned
forever in your amber.

Surely it must be so. I sweep aside as so much protective
persiflage the protests of those cartoonists I know personally
that theirs is in fact a life of sweat, tears and trauma, of nail-
biting rejection, of long years of arduous apprenticeship,
finger cramps and red-eyed midnight toil. Obviously, they
want to camoflauge their blissful haven with a net of flimsy
difficulties, trials and tribulations lest others break in and spoil
Eden.

To wax profound on the subject of humor is right in there
with throwing newly-hatched robins out of their nest in the
interest of teaching them to fly. But it is my ponderous
conviction that cartoons are the poetry of humor — catching
and distilling the instant of human folly with carefully
rendered lines which convey a universal — if not always
earthshaking — revelation.

The best cartoons of all are those that need no captions, but if such stringent limitation were imposed we would be deprived of the many classics which require a line or two at the tip of their spear. Good captions have a poetic economy — one word too many can blunt them into banality. Like the poet, the cartoonist must have a good ear as well as a ravenous eye.

I believe, too, that cartoonists are born, not made. And, while I can discern no reason why it should be so, that cartooning is primarily a male province; also, unlike many other creative talents, it is one that almost universally improves with age and practice.

All these wonderful things cartoonists are, then, and in almost fifteen years of working with cartoonists from Europe and the U.S., I have found them to be among the most pleasant, reliable and urbane of people. It may be that they feel they must be so civil in order to disguise their uniqueness. For, while comedians and gag-writers may actually sit around and think up jokes, I am fairly confident that a good cartoonist actually sees the world from some angle or skewed vantage point closed to most mere mortals.

It's a gift that perhaps can be cultivated or ignored, maybe even turned off and on at will, but it's not something that can be learned or taught.

Four of the five artists whose work is presented in this book drawn from the pages of *The Critic* magazine have managed to achieve the Nirvana of full-time cartooning. Only Charles Healy must still bear the cross of employment — but shed no tears for him since he labors in the advertising business, which many consider to be even cushier. Bill Tidy is perhaps Britain's best-known cartoonist, a *Punch* veteran of prodigious output and talent. The work of Joseph Farris and Sidney

Harris is equally outstanding and visible in the U.S.; Rodrigues (who will permit his first name to appear only on checks) is the creator of the syndicated comic strip *Casey*; his dark perceptions and less than benevolent eye have long ago earned him a national following.

Since *The Critic* is a publication of both religious and cultural orientation, many — though by no means all — of the cartoons herein reflect that bias. Mixing religion and humor can be the most dangerous game because many consider the merest hint of a smile or snicker in this area nothing less than sacrilege. If you doubt this, I invite you to glance through the thick sheaf of positively venemous letters of denunciation which have been directed at us over the years. If you count yourself among that dour band, please put down this book at once. I have long since given up trying to convert people to the most reasonable view that just as many funny, absurd and outrageous things happen in and to the Church — which after all is not composed of angels — as in any other area where mortals gather. In fact, in matters so solemn and which have a way of funding themselves with built-in awe, the chances to take oneself too seriously, to speak pompously and to behave fatuously rise spectacularly. Religious people, in fact, may need the therapeutic power of humor more than most.

To those who agree that to err is human, to forgive divine and to laugh is what you do in between, this book is happily dedicated.

Joel Wells
Editor, *The Critic*

Bill Tidy

Born 1933 in Cheshire. Moved to Liverpool for the Blitz. Survived. Left school at 15, and worked in a shipping office, then joined the army. Served three years in Germany, Korea and Japan. Gave first cartoon to a Japanese newspaper. Then back to an advertising agency in Liverpool.

Took up cartooning in 1957. Now live in Southport with Neapolitan wife and three children.

Contributed to *Punch, Private Eye* ("The Cloggies"), *Daily Mirror* ("The Fosdyke Sage"), B.B.C. and I.T.V., Advertising Agencies and everyone else.

Received Granada T.V. "What the Papers Say" award for Cartoonist of the Year 1974.

Bill Tidy

"Well, Jane, it was fun while it lasted."

"I know you're a craftsman, Ali, but we
had to go over to plastic sometime!"

"What a fantastic, incredible old man.
He said to go somewhere else and kill lots of people."

"Rex!"

"I came as soon as I
got your wire, Mama."

"You were a great disappointment
to your Father, Toni. . . ."

"I'm sorry, Mama.
What actually happened?"

"Look at your brothers and sister!"

"He was crushed by a fall of prayerbooks!"

"You're doing a great job, John, but take it easy!"

"Carry your bags, sir?"

"Congratulations! You're the first living man
to be made a saint."

"Hey fellows! Come and have a look at this!"

"Father Ramirez. . .No coaching, please!"

"Hold the punch line, Ericson, it's the Padre."

"Have faith, my son, have faith!"

"Don't wander too far, folks. . .We leave at 2:30 sharp!"

"This is rather unusual, Father Nitti--
we usually provide the candidate for canonization."

"Now remember, don't look down and you'll be o.k."

"Blast, that's 500 lire we owe him!"

Charles Healy

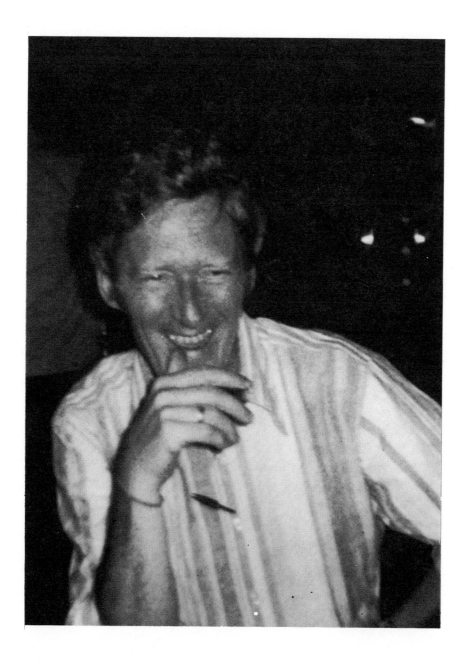

Charles Healy was born in Bridgeport, Connecticut, the eleventh of thirteen children. (Now that they are all grown, he is the eleventh of thirteen adults.)

He studied for the priesthood at Holy Ghost College in Pennsylvania and St. Bonaventure University in New York but gave it up when he realized his vocation extended only to sub-diaconate.

He then enjoyed a tremendous popularity as a high school English teacher because he bore a striking resemblance to George Hamilton IV, a popular pop singer of the day. However, when Mr. Hamilton's popularity declined so did Mr. Healy's and he went into a deep depression and from there into advertising.

It was while he was working at Batten, Barton, Durstine and Osborn Advertising in New York City that Mr. Healy had his first short stories and cartoons published in *The Critic.*

In 1961 he married Diana Dixon in the cathedral in Aachen, Germany. They now have three sons, Douglas, Eric and Jason and they live in Wilton, Conn.

Recently Mr. Healy left BBD & O to become a partner in a new advertising agency. His partner is best known as the man who wrote "Ring around the collar." Mr. Healy is best known as the man who did not write "Ring around the collar."

The new agency's offices are on the 65th floor of the Chrysler Building and Mr. Healy claims that when he stands in the window enjoying the view, people in the street often look up and remark, "That guy up there looks like an ant!"

Charles Healy

"Just for the hell of it,
let's make a motion to ordain women."

HEALY

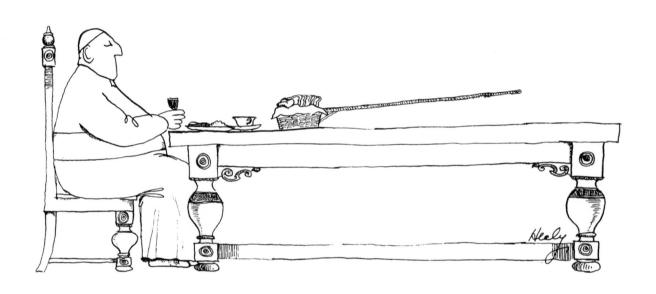

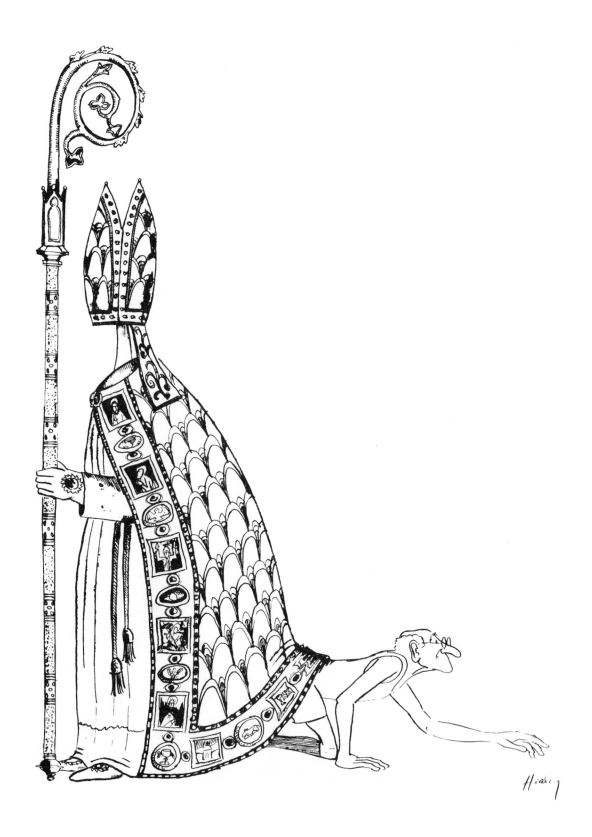

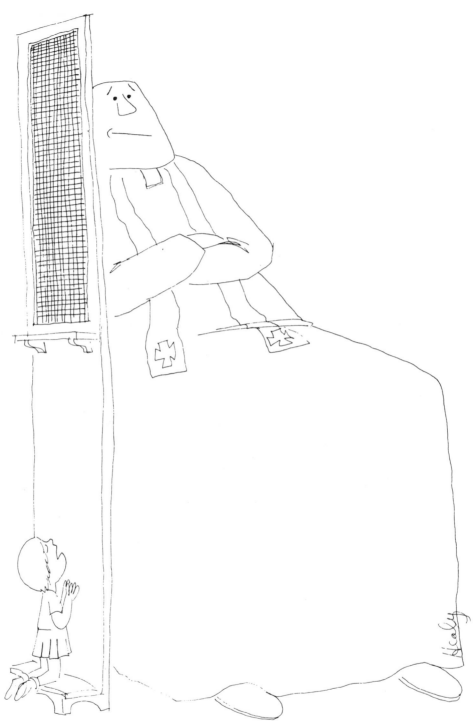

"...I had strange gods and I took
the name of the Lord my God in vain,
and I didn't keep holy the Sabbath,
I didn't honor my mother and father..."

HEALY

"Do you mind if I go first?"

"I'm sorry, but I never discuss religion."

"And to all those who helped us with the bazaar,
I want to say thank you from the bottom. . .

. . .of my heart."

Joseph Farris

I was born on May 30th, 1924 in Newark, N.J. and the first sounds I heard were of a parade, undoubtedly celebrating my arrival. It is now called Memorial Day and is held in my honor.

My childhood was spent in Danbury, Conn. working in my parents' confectionary store where customers interfered with my drawing time. At the age of fourteen or so, the local paper carried an item to the effect that the famous cartoonist Richard Taylor would be giving free art classes in the adjoining town of Bethel. I determined that my budget could afford the free fee and enrolled. Since my time was quite limited, I soon found that I had to choose between the Boy Scouts of America, of which I was a member, and art. Fortunately for the Boy Scouts, I chose art. I soon became good friends with R. Taylor and was greatly influenced by his casual and creative lifestyle. I've never held a job or worked for anyone else except for the period that I worked in my parents' store. On the other hand, I never enjoyed the luxury of complete leisure and an unemployment check.

At 18, I was drafted into the U.S. Army and, after infantry basic training, was soon in the Army Specialized Training Program (ASTP) and sent to The Citadel in Charleston, S.C. in the hope of making an engineer of me. The program was eventually dismantled and it was decided that I was more valuable as an infantryman. I served in the 100th Infantry Division in France and Germany as a heavy machine gunner, squad and section leader. As one of three survivors in my platoon, I was delighted to be a civilian again after almost three years of service.

I attended the Whitney School of Art in New Haven, Conn. for four years as a fine arts student and sold my first drawing, while in school, to the *New York Times* which was a considerable thrill at the time.

My home is high on a hill with a virgin view and a 1000 foot driveway consisting of curves and hills. I spend a good part of the winter plowing the driveway with my trusty jeep.

When I'm not maintaining the place, I work in my studio which is located a short distance from the house atop a two-car garage. My wife, Cynthia, is an elementary art school teacher and between us we have a daughter (mine) and three sons (hers). I'm under contract to the *New Yorker* which has first refusal rights on my cartoons and my work appears in many other publications.

I'm also a painter and have had a one-man show in New York City. The gallery closed down after my show which was reviewed in the *New York Herald Tribune*. The *Herald Tribune* also closed down the next day. I'm now an untouchable.

There's nothing else I'd rather do than cartooning-painting with the possible exception of being a very successful author who works only three hours in the morning. I enjoy being a cartoonist and having, for the most part, control of my life.

Joseph Farris

"Hi. I'm a Jesus Freak, too."

"Dad, who was Nixon?"

"Of course you're big and clumsy but don't forget
one thing: you're supposed to be big and clumsy."

"You mean we've <u>all</u> forgotten the formula
for making our secret liqueur?"

"What a relief! We were afraid your form of life
would be vastly different than ours!"

"Nasty, right to the end!"

"Well, nobody can break in.
The only trouble is that I'm afraid to go out."

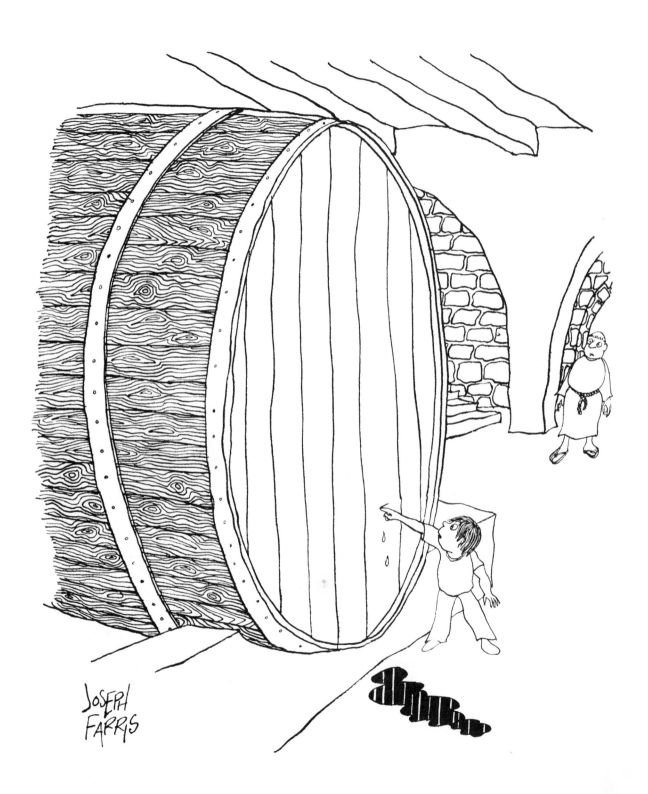

"At this moment, He is in conference. At the beep, you will have sixty seconds to say your prayers. . . . This is a recording. . . ."

JOSEPH FARRIS

Rodrigues

MY MOTHER SAID I WAS BORN 51 YEARS AGO IN NEW BEDFORD, MASSACHUSETTS. (SEE, I STARTED A BIOGRAPHICAL SKETCH WITHOUT `I´!)

I AM OF PORTUGUESE ANCESTRY AS WAS JOHN DOS PASSOS AND MAGELLAN. I AM MARRIED - HAVE TWO DAUGHTERS AND LIVE CLOSE BY CAPE COD.

MY PUBLIC SCHOOL EDUCATION STOPPED AT THE EIGHTH GRADE WHEN I LEFT TO LEARN HOW TO APPLY PAINT TO VENETIAN BLINDS. A YEAR LATER AT 17 I JOINED THE U.S. NAVY. FOLLOWING MY HONOURABLE (I'M ALSO AN ANGLOPHILE) DISCHARGE I TOOK UP CARTOONING AND WAS REALLY LOUSY AT IT. NOW I'M GETTING A LITTLE BETTER AT IT.

CURRENTLY THE BULK OF MY CARTOONING INVOLVES MY SYNDICATED COMIC STRIP `CASEY´ I ALSO WORK REGULARLY FOR `THE NATIONAL LAMPOON´ AND `STEREO REVIEW´. I DO MOST OF MY WORK AT NIGHT. WITH ME IT'S A SEVEN DAYS A WEEK EFFORT. WORKING ON THE SABBATH DID BOTHER ME AND I CONSULTED A FRANCISCAN PRIEST WHO ASSURED ME THAT CREATIVE EFFORTS WERE EXEMPT AND THAT I SHOULD GO TO IT AND MAKE A LOT OF MONEY.

LISTENING TO CLASSICAL MUSIC IS MY AVOCATION - FROM CHAMBER TO SYMPHONIC. THIS DOES NOT PRECLUDE MY LIKING FOR 1930ISH POPULAR MUSIC. RAY NOBLE, RUSS COLUMBO, BING CROSBY AND HOLLYWOOD MUSICAL SOUND TRACKS - RUBY KEELER, DICK POWELL AND EVEN GEORGE JESSEL SINGING. `MY MOTHER'S EYES´.

MY READING IS CURIOUS - AGATHA CHRISTIE, SINCLAIR LEWIS, HENRY THOREAU, THE AFOREMENTIONED JOHN DOS PASSOS AND SOLZHENITSYN AMONG OTHERS. MY MAINSTAY HAS TO BE BIOGRAPHIES. I SUSPECT THAT A SUCCESSFUL BIOGRAPHER IS ONE WHO TAKES A COURSE IN APOCHRYPHA. I RECALL READING A BIOGRAPHY OF ISADORA DUNCAN WRITTEN BY HER FORMER PERSONAL SECRETARY. SHE CAME OUT A FEW NOTCHES ABOVE SAINT JOAN WHEN IN TRUTH SHE WAS A TALENTED, NAIVE, UNDISCIPLINED, LAZY, PRETENTIOUS FREELOADER.

I ASLO HATE GORE VIDAL!

RODRIGUES

"...Men, I'm Joseph Braithwaite your new warden--we might get off to a good start by understanding that I don't hold much to the bleeding-heart philosophy of penology..."

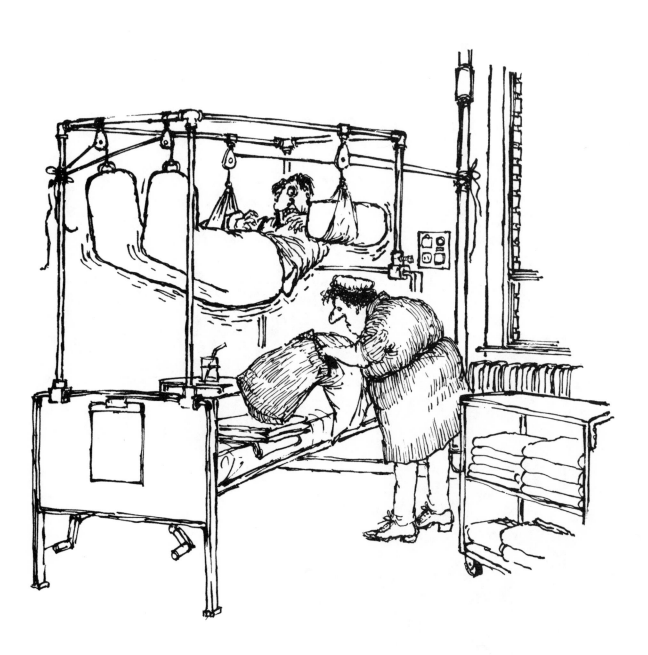

"Oh, I just know it's bad news!"

"...Larry, How are you?--This is Virginia Barr;
Listen, Larry, now, no cheating, <u>Promise</u>?
I'm putting on a 'Come as you are' party..."

". . .You up there! I am Dr. Bernard Gelb, a psychiatrist. I am going to say a series
of words and to each I want you to respond with the first thing that enters your mind."

"He comes over three days every month from St. Anthony's Roman Catholic Cathedral as part of our community ecumenical program."

". . . I'm sorry, Sir, you can't read erotic books while we're in Irish air space. . ."

"...That really isn't necessary, Mrs. Lentz,
J. Spaeth Sons services are quite adequate..."

"Gerald and I discussed it thoroughly and agreed
that artificial insemination was the best course. . ."

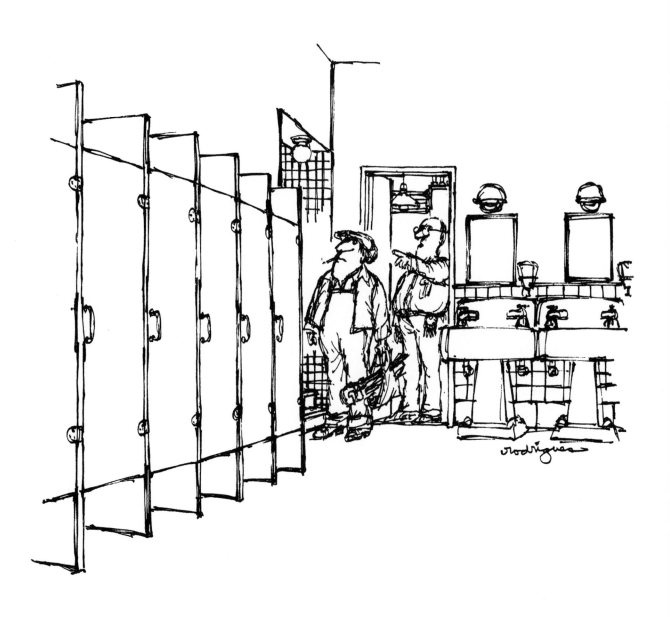

". . .Look for the one that has the quote from Kafka
on the inside of the door--that's the one that has the leak. . ."

Sidney Harris

My alter ego happened to be passing by just as I sat down to do this piece, and he offered to interview my ego. Knowing I couldn't do any better, I accepted the offer.

AE: This place is a mess. I take it you've drawn quite a few cartoons.

E: Yes, I've done several thousand over a period of more than twenty years — although it sometimes seems like twenty cartoons over a period of several thousand years.

AE: I suppose you know the reason for doing all of this, or, to paraphrase Freud, "What do cartoonists want?"

E: My original motivation, if I remember correctly, was to kill a few hours each day, but now I could do that by looking out of the window.

AE: Which, as I understand it . . . .

E: Yes, that takes up a good part of a freelance's day. In my case I spend the first few hours of every morning looking for the mailman. If he happens to arrive early, I still look for him, hoping, I suppose, that he will reappear with tomorrow's mail.

AE: Then, I suppose, you get down to the major work of cartooning, which is drawing those little pictures.

E: Not exactly. There is always some mail to answer, some photocopies to be made, and some more windows to look through. Thus a full working day can go by without drawing, which, in any case, is so much drudgery.

AE: What else does it take to be a cartoonist?

E: Fortunately,.I have two important traits: a continual case of writer's block, and a short attention span. Both can be relieved for a minute or so by coming up with an idea or caption.

AE: I've heard the propensity for humor runs in families.
E: Very likely. I've inherited a great deal from my wife, who makes sculptures which are witty and incisive, and from my two children, who are always ad libbing.

AE: I suppose you'd like to get in a plug now.
E: Well, three books of my cartoons have been published in the past few years (*So Far, So Good,* Playboy Press, 1971; *Pardon Me, Miss,* Dell, 1973 and *What's So Funny About Science?,* William Kaufmann, Inc. 1977) but I don't believe any of them contain the great American cartoon. Perhaps the quest for this white whale of humor is the motivation for the whole thing.

Sidney Harris

"My son, according to our Databank,
you did the same thing four years ago."

"Could you indicate to us somehow
what compelled you to take a vow of silence?"

"Get a bishop!"

"The question remains--when Charlie saw St. Francis,
was he under the influence or wasn't he?"

"You go up, you come down. You go up, you come
down. This reincarnation is a pain in the neck!"

"Because it can be expressed in so many ways--sado-masochism, passion, bondage, sodomy--I'd say lust is my favorite."

VIOLATORS WILL
BE PROSECUTED

"That lumbago you just got rid
of--you gave it to me."

"Darling--our mixed
marriage isn't mixed
any longer. I've
become Jewish."

"But I've just
become Catholic."

"It happened this morning."

"Father Abbot doesn't understand me!"

"So much for our carefree, puckish way of life."

"Women's Lib? What Women's Lib?"

"If you don't mind, you seem to be sitting on my brother."

"Probably at first it will be one diocese--
but the moon is a big place."